contents

To Learn by Video for these patterns, please visit
www.go-crafty.com/1-hour-dishcloths-to-crochet

For pattern inquiries, please visit: www.go-crafty.com

scrubbie posy dishcloth

YARN
Lily® Sugar'n Cream® (Solids 2.5 oz/70.9 g; 120 yds/109 m)
- 1 ball or 10½ yds/9.5 m each in #01215 Robin's Egg or #00071 Grape or #01699 Tangerine or #01740 Hot Pink (A)
- 1 ball or 7½ yds/6.5 m each in #01740 Hot Pink or #01699 Tangerine or #01712 Hot Green or #01223 Mod Green (B)

HOOKS
Sizes E/4 and G/6 (3.5 and 4 mm) crochet hooks *or size needed to obtain gauge*

ADDITIONAL
Plastic scrubby appox 3¼" [8.5 cm] diameter

LEARN BY VIDEO
www.go-crafty.com
- ch (chain)
- Crocheting in the round
- dc
- sc
- sl st (slip stitch)
- tr

MEASUREMENTS
Approx 8½" [21.5 cm] diameter.

GAUGE
14 sc and 15 rows = 4" [10 cm] with larger hook. *Take time to check gauge.*

NOTE
Scrubbie may be worked from text or chart.

INSTRUCTIONS
1st rnd: With RS of plastic scrubbie facing, A and smaller hook, work 36 sc evenly around outer edge of scrubbie, working each sc around 3 or 4 strands of plastic scrubbie. Join with sl st to first sc.
Change to larger hook.
2nd rnd: Ch 1. 1 sc in same sp as last sl st. *Ch 5. Skip next 2 sc. 1 sc in next sc. Rep from * around, ending with ch 5. Skip last 2 sc. Join with sl st to first sc.
3rd rnd: Sl st in first ch-5 sp. Ch 3 (counts as dc). (2 dc. 3 tr. 3 dc) in same sp. *1 sc in next ch-5 sp. (3 dc. 3 tr. 3 dc) in next ch-5 sp. Rep from * around, ending with 1 sc in last ch-5 sp. Join with sl st to top of ch 3. Fasten off. 6 petals.
4th rnd: Join B with sl st in center tr of any petal. Ch 1. (1 sc. *Ch 3. Sl st in last sc worked*—picot made. 1 sc) in same sp as last sl st. 1 sc in each of next 4 sts. *[Yoh and draw up a loop in next skipped sc from 2nd rnd (working around 3rd rnd). Yoh and draw through 2 loops on hook] twice. Yoh and draw through all loops on hook— spike st made. 1 sc in each of next 4 sts.** (1 sc. Picot. 1 sc) in next tr. 1 sc in each of next 4 sts. Rep from * 4 times more, then from * to ** once. Join with sl st to first sc. Fasten off.

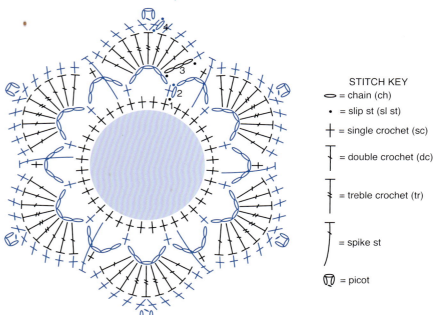

Scrubby

STITCH KEY
◯ = chain (ch)
• = slip st (sl st)
+ = single crochet (sc)
╤ = double crochet (dc)
╤ = treble crochet (tr)
╤ = spike st
⬡ = picot

gotta wear shades dishcloth

YARN
Lily® Sugar'n Cream® (Solids 2.5 oz/70.9 g; 120 yds/109m)
- 1 ball or 90 yds/80 m in #00073 Sunshine (MC),
- 1 ball or 7 yds/6 m in #00095 Red (A)
- 1 ball or 11 yd/10 m in #00002 in Black (C)

Note: 1 ball of MC will make 2 dishcloths

HOOKS
Sizes G/6 and H/8 (4 mm and 5 mm) crochet hooks *or size needed to obtain gauge*

ADDITIONAL
Tapestry needle

LEARN BY VIDEO
www.go-crafty.com
- ch (chain)
- Crocheting in the round
- dc
- hdc
- sc
- sc2tog
- sl st (slip stitch)
- tr

MEASUREMENTS
Approx 10" [25.5 cm] in diameter.

GAUGE
13 sc and 14 rows = 4" [10 cm] with larger hook. *Take time to check gauge.*

NOTES
1 Sun may be worked from text or chart.
2 Ch 2 at beg of rnd does not count as st.

SPECIAL STITCHES
dtr (Yoh) 3 times and draw up a loop in next stitch. (Yoh and draw through 2 loops on hook) 4 times.

INSTRUCTIONS
Sun

With larger hook and MC, ch 3.

1st rnd: 10 hdc in 3rd ch from hook. Join with sl st to first hdc. 10 hdc.

2nd rnd: Ch 2. 2 hdc in each hdc around. Join with sl st to first hdc. 20 hdc.

3rd rnd: Ch 2. *2 hdc in next hdc. 1 hdc in next hdc. Rep from * around. Join with sl st to first hdc. 30 hdc.

4th rnd: Ch 2. *2 hdc in next hdc. 1 hdc in each of next 2 hdc. Rep from * around. Join with sl st to first hdc. 40 hdc.

5th rnd: Ch 2. *2 hdc in next hdc. 1 hdc in each of next 3 hdc. Rep from * around. Join with sl st to first hdc. 50 hdc.

6th rnd: Ch 2. *2 hdc in next hdc. 1 hdc in each of next 4 hdc. Rep from * around. Join with sl st to first hdc. 60 hdc.

7th rnd: Ch 2. *2 hdc in next hdc. 1 hdc in each of next 5 hdc. Rep from * around. Join with sl st to first hdc. 70 hdc.

8th rnd: Ch 2. *(2 hdc in next hdc. 1 hdc in each of next 8 hdc) 7 times. 2 hdc in next hdc. 1 hdc in each of next 6 hdc. Join with sl st to first hdc. 78 hdc.

9th rnd: Ch 1. 1 sc in same sp as sl st. *Ch 7. 1 sc in 2nd ch from hook. 1 hdc in next ch. 1 dc in next ch. 1 tr in next ch. 1 dtr in next ch. (Yoh) 4 times and draw up a loop in next ch. (Yoh and draw up a loop through 2 loops on hook) 5 times—triple tr (tr tr) made. Skip next

5 hdc of 8th rnd.** 1 sc in next hdc. Rep from * 11 times more, then from * to ** once. Join with sl st to first sc. Fasten off.

SUNGLASSES
Lens (make 2)
With B and smaller hook, ch 9.
1st row: 1 sc in 2nd ch from hook. 1 sc in each ch to end of chain. Turn. 8 sc.
2nd to 5th rows: Ch 1. 1 sc in each sc to end of row. Turn.
6th row: Ch 1. Sc2tog. (1 sc in next sc. Sc2tog) twice. 5 sts. Do not turn.

Edging
1st rnd: Ch 1. Work 1 rnd of sc evenly around Lens, having 3 sc in each corner. Join A with sl st to first sc.
2nd rnd: With A, ch 1. Work 1 sc in each sc around, having 2 sc in each corner. Join with sl st to first sc. Fasten off.

Join Lenses
1st row: Join A with sl st to top left of first Lens. Ch 1. 1 sc in each of next 3 sc. Turn.
2nd row: Ch 1. 1 sc in each of next 3 sc. Fasten off, leaving a long end. Thread end through tapestry needle. Sew last row to corresponding sc of Second Lens.

FINISHING
Sew Sunglasses to Sun as shown in picture. With B, embroider smile using back stitch. ■

Backstitch

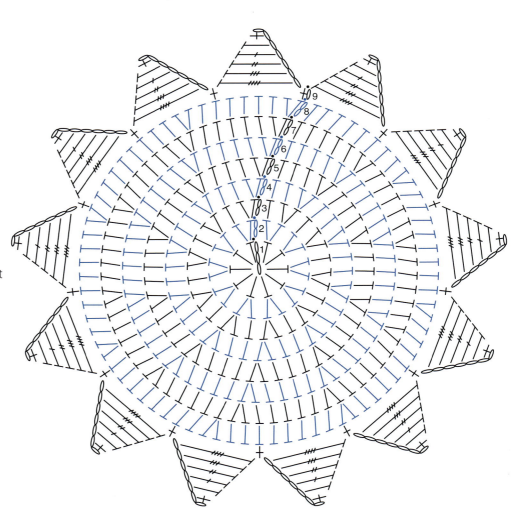

vintage blossom dishcloth

YARN (4)
Lily® Sugar'n Cream® (Solids 2.5 oz/70.9 g; 120 yds/109 m)
- 1 ball or 17 yds/15 m in #01222 Country Green (A)
- 1 ball or 18 yds/16 m in #01215 Robin's Egg (B)
- 1 ball or 22 yds/20 m in #01699 in Tangerine (C)
- 1 ball or 19 yds/17 m in #01004 in Soft Ecru (D)

HOOK
Size H/8 (5 mm) crochet hook *or size needed to obtain gauge*

LEARN BY VIDEO
www.go-crafty.com
- ch (chain)
- Crocheting in the round
- dc
- sc
- sl st (slip stitch)

MEASUREMENTS
Approx 8" [20.5 cm] in diameter.

GAUGE
13 sc and 14 rows = 4" [10 cm].
Take time to check gauge.

NOTES
1 Dishcloth can be worked following text or chart.
2 Ch 3 at beg of rnd counts as dc throughout.

INSTRUCTIONS
With A, ch 4. Join with sl st to first ch to form ring.
1st rnd: Ch 3. 11 dc in ring. Join B with sl st to top of ch 3. 12 dc.

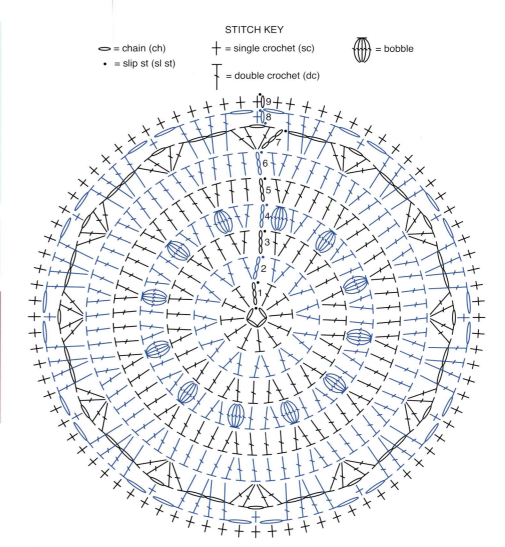

STITCH KEY
◦ = chain (ch)
• = slip st (sl st)
T = double crochet (dc)
+ = single crochet (sc)
🪀 = bobble

2nd rnd: With B, ch 3. 1 dc in same sp as last sl st. *2 dc in next dc. Rep from * around. Join A with sl st to top of ch 3. 24 dc.
3rd rnd: With A, ch 3. *2 dc in next dc. 1 dc in next dc. Rep from * around. Join C with sl st to top of ch 3. 36 dc.
4th rnd: With C, ch 3. 2 dc in next dc. (Yoh and draw up a loop. Yoh and draw through 2 loops on hook) 5 times in next dc. Yoh and draw through 6 loops on hook (bobble made). *1 dc in next dc. 2 dc in next dc. Bobble in next dc. Rep from * around. Join B with sl st to top of ch 3. 48 sts.
5th rnd: With B, ch 3. 1 dc in each of next 2 sts. 2 dc in next st. *1 dc in each of next 3 sts. 2 dc in next st. Rep from * around. Join D with sl st to top of ch 3. 60 dc.
6th rnd: With D, ch 3. 1 dc in each of next 3 dc. 2 dc in next dc. *1 dc in each of next 4 dc. 2 dc in next dc. Rep from * around. Join C with sl st to top of ch 3. 72 dc.
7th rnd: With C, ch 3. (1 dc. Ch 1. 2 dc) all in same sp as last sl st. *Ch 2. Skip next 5 dc. (2dc. Ch 1. 2dc) in next dc. Rep from * around, ending with skip last 5 dc. Join with sl st to top of ch 3. Fasten off.

8th rnd: Join D with sl st to any ch-1 sp. Ch 1. 1 sc in same sp as last sl st. *Ch 1. Working in front of ch 2 and into 6th rnd, skip next dc. 1 dc in next dc. 2 dc in next dc. 1 dc in next dc. Skip next dc. Ch 1. 1 sc in next ch-1sp of 7th rnd. Rep from * around, ending with ch 1. Join A with sl st to first sc.

9th rnd: With A, ch 1. 1 sc in same sp as last sl st. *1 sc in next ch-1 sp. 1 sc in each of next 4 dc. 1 sc in next ch-1 sp. 1 sc in next sc. Rep from * around, omitting sc at end of last rep. Join with sl st to first sc. 84 sc. Fasten off. ■

apple a day dishcloth

YARN
Lily® Sugar'n Cream® (Solids 2.5 oz/70.9 g; 120 yds/109m)
- 1 ball each in #00004 Ecru (MC); #01530 Country Red or #01712 Hot Green (A); #01130 Warm Brown (B); and #00084 Sage Green (C)

HOOK
Size G/6 (4 mm) crochet hook
or size needed to obtain gauge

LEARN BY VIDEO
www.go-crafty.com
- **ch (chain)**
- **Crocheting in the round**
- dc
- hdc
- sc
- sl st (slip stitch)
- tr

MEASUREMENTS
Approx 8" [20.5 cm] in diameter.

GAUGE
15 sc and 16 rows = 4" [10 cm].
Take time to check gauge.

NOTE
Ch 3 at beg of rnd or row counts as dc.

INSTRUCTIONS
Apple
With MC, ch 4. Join with sl st to form ring.
1st rnd: Ch 3. 11 dc in ring. Join with sl st to top of ch 3. 12 dc.
2nd rnd: Ch 3.1 dc in same sp as last sl st. 2 dc in each dc around. Join with sl st to top of ch 3. 24 dc.
3rd rnd: Ch 3. 2 dc in next dc. *1 dc in next dc. 2 dc in next dc. Rep from* around. Join with sl st to top of ch 3. 36 dc.
4th rnd: Ch 3. 1 dc in next dc. 2 dc in next dc. *1 dc in each of next 2 dc. 2 dc in next dc. Rep from * around. Join with sl st to top of ch 3. 48 dc.
5th rnd: Ch 3. 1 dc in same sp as last sl st. 1 dc in each of next 3 dc. *2 dc in next dc. 1 dc in each of next 3 dc. Rep from * around. Join with sl st to top of ch 3. 60 dc.
6th rnd: Ch 1. 1 sc in each of next 3 dc. 1 hdc in next dc. 1 dc in next dc. (2 dc in next dc. 1 dc in next dc) 4 times. 1 hdc in next dc. 1 sc in each of next 6 dc. 1 hdc in next dc. 1 dc in each of next 2 dc. 2 dc in each of next 3 dc. 1 dc in next dc. 1 hdc in next dc. 1 sc in next dc. Sl st in each of next 2 dc. 1 sc in next dc. 1 hdc in next dc. 1 dc in next dc. 2 dc in each of next 3 dc. 1 dc in each of next 2 dc. 1 hdc in next dc. 1 sc in each of next 6 dc. 1 hdc in next dc. (1 dc in next dc. 2 dc in next dc) 4 times. 1 dc in next dc. 1 hdc in next dc. 1 sc in each of next 3 dc. Join A with sl st to first sc. 74 sts. Break MC.
7th rnd: With A, ch 1. 1 sc in same sp as last sl st. 1 hdc in next sc. 1 dc in each of next 4 sts. (2 dc in next st. 1 dc in each of next 5 sts) 4 times. 2 dc in next st. 1 dc in each of next 4 sts. 1 hdc in next st. 1 sc in each of next 2 sts. 1 hdc in next st. 1 dc in each of next 4 sts. (2 dc in next st. 1 dc in each of next 5 sts) 4 times. 2 dc in next st. 1 dc in each of next 4 sts. 1 hdc in next st. 1 sc in next st. Join with sl st to first sc. Fasten off.

Hanging Loop
With 2 strands of B held tog, join with sl st to top of Apple. Ch 12. Join with sl st in same sp as first sl st. Fasten off.

Bullion Stitch

Leaf

With C, ch 12.

1st row: 1 sc in 2nd ch from hook. 1 hdc in next ch. 1 dc in next ch. 1 tr in each of next 5 ch. 1 dc in next ch. 1 hdc in next ch. 3 sc in last ch. Working across opposite side of ch, 1 hdc in next ch. 1 dc in next ch. 1 tr in each of next 5 ch. 1 dc in next ch. 1 hdc in next ch. 2 sc in last ch. Join with sl st to first sc. Fasten off.

FINISHING

Sew Leaf to Apple near Hanging Loop. With B, embroider seeds using Bullion st using photo as a guide. ∎

chrysanthemum dishcloth

YARN
Lily® Sugar'n Cream® (Solids 2.5 oz/70.9 g; 120 yds/109 m)
Version 1
- 1 ball each in #01628 Hot Orange (MC) and #00001 White (A)

Version 2
- 1 ball each in #00073 Sunshine (MC) and #02741 Playtime (A)

Version 3
- 1 ball each in #00073 Sunshine (MC) and #02743 Summer Splash (A)

HOOK
Size H/8 (5 mm) crochet hook
or size needed to obtain gauge

LEARN BY VIDEO
www.go-crafty.com
- ch (chain)
- Crocheting in the round
- dc
- hdc
- sc
- sl st (slip stitch)

MEASUREMENTS
Approx 10" [25.5 cm] in diameter.

GAUGE
13 sc and 14 rows = 4" [10 cm].
Take time to check gauge.

NOTE
Ch 2 does not count as hdc in 1st to 3rd rnds.

INSTRUCTIONS
With MC, ch 4. Join with sl st to first ch to form a ring.

1st rnd: Ch 2. 10 hdc in ring. Join with sl st to first hdc.

2nd rnd: Ch 2. 2 hdc in each hdc around. Join with sl st to first hdc. 20 hdc.

3rd rnd: Ch 2. 2 hdc in each hdc around. Join with sl st to first hdc. 40 hdc.

4th rnd: Ch 2. (1 hdc. Ch 1. 2 hdc) in same sp as sl st. *Skip next 2 hdc. (2 hdc. Ch 1. 2 hdc) in next hdc. Rep from * around. Join with sl st to top of ch 2.

5th rnd: Sl st in next st and ch-1 sp. Ch 2. (1 hdc. Ch 1. 2 hdc) in same ch-1 sp. *(2 hdc. Ch 1. 2 hdc) in next ch-1 sp (shell made). Rep from * around. Join with sl st to top of ch 2.

6th and 7th rnds: Sl st in next st and ch-1 sp. Ch 2. (2 hdc. Ch 1. 3 hdc) in same ch-1 sp. *(3 hdc. Ch 1. 3 hdc) in next ch-1 sp. Rep from * around. Join A with sl st to top of ch 2 at end of 7th rnd.

8th rnd: With A, ch 2. *8 dc in next ch-1 sp. 1 sc in sp between 2 shells. Rep from * around. Join with sl st to first dc.

9th rnd: Ch 1. 1 sc in same sp as sl st. Ch 1. (1 sc in next dc. Ch 1) 7 times. *(1 sc in sp between next 2 shells 1 row below. Ch 1) 4 times. 1 sc in same ch-1 sp as last sc. (Ch 1. 1 sc in sp between next 2 shells 1 row above) 3 times.** (1 sc in next dc. Ch 1) 8 times. Rep from * 11 times more, then from * to ** once. Join with sl st to first sc. Fasten off. ■

gingham dishcloth

YARN
Lily® Sugar'n Cream® (Solids 2.5 oz/70.9 g; 120 yds/109 m)
- 1 ball each in #01004 Soft Ecru (MC), #01116 Blue Jeans (A), and #00009 Bright Navy (B)

HOOK
Size G/6 (4 mm) crochet hook *or size needed to obtain gauge*

LEARN BY VIDEO
www.go-crafty.com
- ch (chain)
- Changing colors
- sc
- sl st (slip stitch)

MEASUREMENTS
Approx 9½" x 9½" [24 cm x 24 cm].

GAUGE
15 sc and 16 rows = 4" [10 cm].
Take time to check gauge.

NOTES
1 To join new color, work to last 2 loops on hook. Draw new color through last 2 loops then proceed with new color.
2 Carry yarn not in use loosely across top of previous row and work sts around it to prevent stranding.

INSTRUCTIONS
With B, ch 36.

1st row: (RS). 1 sc in 2nd ch from hook. (Ch 1. Skip next ch. 1 sc in next ch) twice. *With A, (1 sc in next ch. Ch 1. Skip next ch) twice. 1 sc in next ch. With MC, (1 sc in next ch. Ch 1. Skip next ch) twice. 1 sc in next ch. Rep from * twice more. 35 sts. Turn.

2nd row: With MC, ch 1. 1 sc in first sc. 1 sc in next ch-1 sp. Ch 1. Skip next sc. 1 sc in next ch-1 sp. 1 sc in next sc. *With A, 1 sc in next sc. 1 sc in next ch-1 sp. Ch 1. Skip next sc. 1 sc in next ch-1 sp. 1 sc in next sc. With MC, 1 sc in next sc. 1 sc in next ch-1 sp. Ch 1. Skip next sc. 1 sc in next ch-1 sp. 1 sc in next sc. Rep from * twice more. Turn.

3rd row: With MC, ch 1. 1 sc in first sc. Ch 1. Skip next sc. 1 sc in next ch-1 sp. Ch 1. Skip next sc. 1 sc in next sc. *With A, 1 sc in next sc. Ch 1. Skip next sc. 1 sc in next ch-1 sp. Ch 1. Skip next sc. 1 sc in next sc. With MC, 1 sc in next sc. Ch 1. Skip next sc. 1 sc in next ch-1 sp. Ch 1. Skip next sc. 1 sc in next sc. Rep from * twice more. Turn.

4th row: As 2nd row. With A, turn.

5th row: With A, ch 1. 1 sc in first sc. Ch 1. Skip next sc. 1 sc in next ch-1 sp. Ch 1. Skip next sc. 1 sc in next sc. *With B, 1 sc in next sc. Ch 1. Skip next sc. 1 sc in next ch-1 sp. Ch 1. Skip next sc. 1 sc in next sc. With A, 1 sc in next sc. Ch 1. Skip next sc. 1 sc in next ch-1 sp. Ch 1. Skip next sc. 1 sc in next sc. Rep from * twice more. Turn.

6th row: With A, ch 1. 1 sc in first sc. 1 sc in next ch-1 sp. Ch 1. Skip next sc. 1 sc in next ch-1 sp. 1 sc in next sc. *With B, 1 sc in next sc. 1 sc in next ch-1 sp. Ch 1. Skip next sc. 1 sc in next ch-1 sp. 1 sc in next sc. With A, 1 sc in next sc. 1 sc in next ch-1 sp. Ch 1. Skip next sc. 1 sc in next ch-1 sp. 1 sc in next sc. Rep from * twice more. Turn.

7th and 8th rows: As 5th and 6th rows, joining MC at end of 8th row.

9th row: As 3rd row.

Rep 2nd to 9th rows for pat 3 times more, then rep 2nd to 4th rows once. Fasten off.

Edging
With RS facing, join B with sl st to any corner. Ch 1. 3 sc in same sp. Work sc evenly around outer edge of Dishcloth, working 3 sc in each corner. Join with sl st to first sc. Fasten off.

spring flower dishcloth

YARN
Lily® Sugar'n Cream® (Solids 2.5 oz/70.9 g; 120 yds/109 m)
- 1 ball each in #00001 White (MC) ; #01712 Hot Green (A) ; #01215 Robin's Egg (B) ; and #00010 Yellow or #00046 Rose Pink (C)

Note: 1 ball each of MC, A, B and C will make 2 dishcloths.

HOOK
Sizes E/4 and G/6 (3.5 and 4 mm) crochet hooks *or size needed to obtain gauge*

ADDITIONAL
Tapestry needle

LEARN BY VIDEO
www.go-crafty.com
- ch (chain)
- Crocheting in the round
- dc
- hdc
- sc (single crochet)
- sl st (slip stitch)
- tr

MEASUREMENTS
Approx 8" [20.5 cm] diameter.

GAUGE
14 sc and 15 rows = 4" [10 cm] with larger hook. *Take time to check gauge.*

NOTE
1 When joining colors, work to last 2 loops on hook of first color. Draw new color through last 2 loops and proceed.
2 When joining a new color, leave a tail approximately 4 inches [10 centimeters] long to ensure you are left with enough yarn to weave in your end.
3 Dishcloth can be worked following text or charts.

INSTRUCTIONS
With B and larger hook, ch 5. Join with sl st in first ch to form ring.

1st rnd: Ch 1. 8 sc in ring. Join with sl st to first sc.

2nd rnd: Ch 1. 2 sc in each sc around. 16 sc. Join MC with sl st to first sc.

3rd rnd: With MC, ch 1. 2 sc in same sp as last sl st. *1 sc in next sc. 2 sc in next sc. Rep from * to last sc. 1 sc in last sc. 24 sc. Join with sl st to first sc.

4th rnd: Ch 3 (counts as dc). 1 dc in same sp as last sl st. *Ch 2. Skip next 2 sc. 2 dc in next sc. Rep from * to last 2 sc. Ch 2. Skip last 2 sc. Join B with sl st to top of ch 3.

5th rnd: With B, ch 1. 1 sc in same sp as last sl st. 1 sc in next dc. *Working in front of next ch-2 sp, 1 tr in each of next 2 skipped sc. 1 sc in each of next 2 dc. Rep from * around, ending with 1 tr in each of last 2 skipped sc. Join C with sl st in first sc.

6th rnd: With C, ch 1. Working in front loops only of each st around, (1 sc. Ch 2. 2 tr) in same sc as last sl st. (2 tr. Ch 2. 1 sc) in next sc. *1 sc in each of next 2 tr. (1 sc. Ch 2. 2 tr) in next sc. (2 tr. Ch 2. 1 sc) in next sc. Rep from * around, ending with 1 sc in each of last 2 tr. Join with sl st to first sc. 8 petals. Break C.

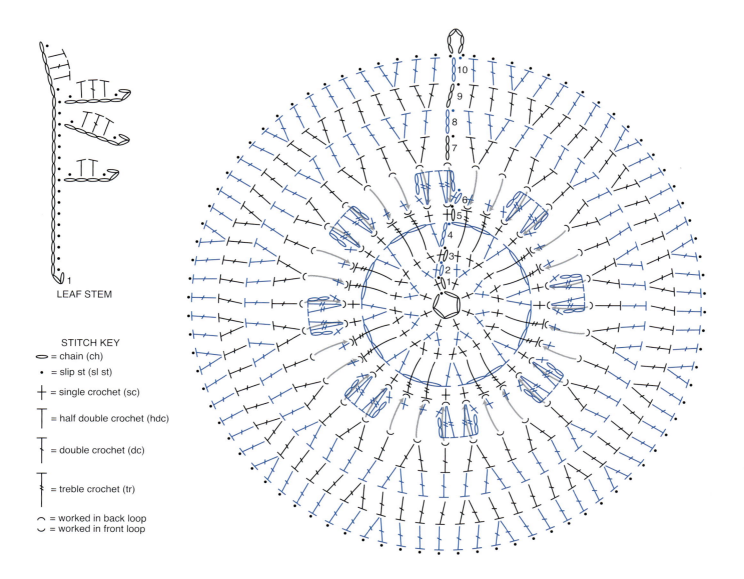

LEAF STEM

STITCH KEY
- ○ = chain (ch)
- • = slip st (sl st)
- + = single crochet (sc)
- T = half double crochet (hdc)
- ┼ = double crochet (dc)
- ╪ = treble crochet (tr)
- ⌒ = worked in back loop
- ⌣ = worked in front loop

7th rnd: Join MC with sl st in any rem back loop of st from last rnd. Ch 3 (counts as dc). Working in rem back loops of each st around, *2 dc in next st. 1 dc in next st. Rep from * around; ending with 2 dc in last st. 48 dc. Join with sl st to top of ch 3.

8th rnd: Ch 3 (counts as dc). 1 dc in next dc. *2 dc in next dc. 1 dc in each of next 3 dc. Rep from * to last 2 dc. 2 dc in next dc. 1 dc in last dc. Join with sl st to top of ch 3. 60 dc.

9th rnd: Ch 3 (counts as dc). *2 dc in next dc. 1 dc in each of next 4 dc. Rep from * to last 4 dc. 2 dc in next dc. 1 dc in each of last 3 dc. Join with sl st to top of ch 3. 72 dc.

10th rnd: Ch 3 (counts as dc). 1 dc in each of next 2 dc. *2 dc in next dc. 1 dc in each of next 5 dc. Rep from * to last 3 dc. 2 dc in next dc. 1 dc in each of last 2 dc. Join B with sl st to top of ch 3. 84 dc.

11th rnd: With B, ch 6 for hanging loop. Sl st in same sp as first sl st. Sl st in each dc around. Join with sl st at base of hanging loop. Fasten off.

Leaf Stem

With A and smaller hook, ch 23.

1st row: Working in back "bumps" of foundation ch, sl st in 3rd ch from hook. Sl st in each of next 8 ch. Ch 6. Sl st in 3rd ch from hook. 1 hdc in each of next 2 ch. Sl st in next ch. Return to original foundation ch, sl st in each of next 5 ch. *Ch 7. Sl st in 3rd ch from hook. 1 hdc in next ch. 1 dc in next ch. 1 hdc in next ch. Sl st in next ch. * Return to original foundation ch, sl st in each of next 2 ch. Rep from * to *. Return to original foundation ch, sl st in next ch. 1 hdc in next ch. 1 dc in next ch. 1 hdc in next ch. Sl st in last ch. Fasten off.

Sew Leaf Stem in position to opposite side of Dishcloth to hanging loop as shown in picture. ■

owl cross stitch **dishcloth**

YARN
Lily® Sugar'n Cream® (Solids 2.5 oz/70.9 g; 120 yds/109 m)
- 1 ball or 109 yds/100 m in #00004 Ecru (MC)
- 1 ball or 27 yds/25 m #00015 Wine (A),
- 1 ball or 66 yds/60 m each in #01530 Country Red (B) and #01699 Tangerine (C)

HOOK
Size G/6 (4 mm) crochet hook *or size needed to obtain gauge*

LEARN BY VIDEO
www.go-crafty.com
- ch (chain)
- reverse sc
- sc
- sl st (slip stitch)

MEASUREMENTS
Approx 9" x 11" [23 x 28 cm].

GAUGE
15 sc and 16 rows = 4" [10 cm].
Take time to check gauge.

NOTE
Ch 3 at beg of rnd or row counts as dc.

INSTRUCTIONS
With MC, ch 31.
1st row: (RS). 1 sc in 2nd ch from hook. 1 sc in each ch to end of chain. 30 sc. Turn.
2nd row: Ch 1. 1 sc in each sc to end of row. Turn.
Rep 2nd row 40 times more. Fasten off.

FINISHING
Using cross st, embroider Chart on RS of Dishcloth.

Edging
1st rnd: With RS facing, join C with sl st in bottom left corner. Ch 1. 3 sc in same sp as sl st. Work 1 rnd of sc evenly around, having 3 sc in each corner. Join A with sl st to first sc. Break C.
2nd rnd: With A, ch 1. Working from left to right instead of from right to left as usual, work 1 reverse sc in each sc around. Fasten off. ■

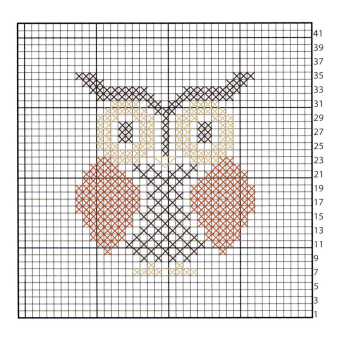

framed posies **dishcloth**

YARN
Lily® Sugar'n Cream® (Solids 2.5 oz/70.9 g; 120 yds/109 m; Ombres 2 oz/56.7 g; 95 yds/86 m)
- 1 ball or 33 yds/30 m in #01699 Tangerine (A)
- 1 ball or 66 yds/60 m each in #01444 Mod Pink (B) and #01712 Hot Green (c)

HOOK
Size H/8 (5 mm) crochet hook *or size needed to obtain gauge*

LEARN BY VIDEO
www.go-crafty.com
- ch (chain)
- Crocheting in the round
- dc
- sl st (slip stitch)

MEASUREMENTS
Approx 9½" x 9½" [24 cm x 24 cm].

GAUGE
13 dc and 7 rows = 4" [10 cm].
Take time to check gauge.

INSTRUCTIONS
Center Section
Top Row
First Flower
With A, ch 4.
1st rnd: [1 dc. Ch 1. 1 dc. Ch 3. Sl st. (Ch 3. 1 dc. Ch 1. 1 dc. Ch 3. Sl st) 3 times] all in 4th ch from hook. Fasten off. 4 petals made.

Second Flower
With B, ch 4.
1st rnd: [(1 dc. Ch 1. 1 dc. Ch 3. Sl st. Ch 3) twice. 1 dc] all in 4th ch from hook. *Drop loop from hook, leaving a long loop. Draw loop through back of ch-1 sp of joining petal of First Flower. Ch 1.* (1 dc. Ch 3. Sl st. Ch 3. 1 dc) in original sp. Rep from * to * once more. (1 dc. Ch 3. Sl st) in original sp. Fasten off. 4 petals made.

Third Flower
With A, as Second Flower, joining petals to Second Flower.

Middle Row
First Flower
With B, as Second Flower of Top Row, joining petals to First Flower of Top Row.

Second Flower
With A, ch 4.
1st rnd: (1 dc. Ch 1. 1 dc. Ch 3. Sl st. Ch 3. 1 dc) all in 4th ch from hook. *Drop loop from hook, leaving a long loop. Draw loop through back of ch-1 sp of joining petal of Second Flower of Top Row. Ch 1. (1 dc. Ch 3. Sl st. Ch 3. 1 dc) in original sp.* Rep from * to * once more. Drop loop from hook, leaving a long loop. Draw loop through back of ch-1 sp of joining petal of First Flower of Middle Row. (1 dc. Ch 3. Sl st) in original sp. Fasten off. 4 petals made.

Third Flower
With B, as Second Flower, joining petals to Third Flower of Top Row and Second Flower of Middle Row.

Bottom Row
First Flower
With A, as Second Flower of Top Row, joining petals to First Flower of Middle Row.

Second Flower
With B, as Second Flower of Middle Row, joining petals to Second Flower of Middle Row and First Flower of Bottom Row.

Third Flower
With A, as Second Flower of Middle Row, joining petals to Third Flower of Middle Row and Second Flower of Bottom Row.

Outer Edging
1st rnd: With RS facing, join C with sl st in back loop of any corner ch-1 sp of Center Section. (Ch 1. 1 sc. Ch 3. 1 sc) in same sp. *(Ch 5. 1 sc in back of joining sp between Flowers) twice. Ch 5.** (1 sc. Ch 3. 1 sc) in back loop of next corner ch-1 sp. Rep from * twice more, then from * to ** once. Join with sl st to first sc.

2nd rnd: Sl st in next ch-3 sp. Ch 3 (counts as dc). (2 dc. Ch 3. 3 dc) all in same sp. *6 dc in next ch-5 sp. 7 dc in next ch-5 sp. 6 dc in next ch-5 sp.** (3 dc. Ch 3. 3 dc) in next corner ch-3 sp. Rep from * twice more, then from * to ** once. Join with sl st to top of ch 3.

3rd rnd: Sl st in next dc. Ch 4 (counts as dc and ch 1). *(3 dc. Ch 3. 3 dc) all in next corner ch-3 sp.** (Ch 1. Skip next dc. 1 dc in next dc) 12 times. Ch 1. Skip next dc. Rep from * twice more, then from * to ** once. (Ch 1. Skip next dc. 1 dc in next dc) 11 times. Ch 1. Skip last dc. Join with sl st to 3rd ch of ch 4.

4th rnd: Ch 3 (counts as dc). 1 dc in next ch-1 sp. *1 dc in each of next 3 dc. (3 dc. Ch 3. 3 dc) all in next corner ch-3 sp. 1 dc in each of next 3 dc. (1 dc in next ch-1 sp. 1 dc in next dc) 12 times. 1 dc in next ch-1 sp. Rep from * twice more. 1 dc in each of next 3 dc. (3 dc. Ch 10. Sl st in 8th ch from hook for hanging loop. Ch 1. 3 dc) all in next corner ch-3 sp. 1 dc in each of next 3 dc. (1 dc in next ch-1 sp. 1 dc in next dc) 12 times. Join with sl st to top of ch 3. Fasten off.

FINISHING
Embroider center of each Flower with French knot using C. ■

French Knot

 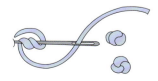

mug of cocoa **dishcloth**

YARN
Lily® Sugar'n Cream® (Solids 2.5 oz/70.9 g; 120 yds/109 m)
- 1 ball or 60 yds/56 m in #01118 Stonewash (A)
- 1 ball or 18 yds/15 m #01130 Warm Brown (B)
- 1 ball or 9 yds/8 m #00001 White (C)

HOOK
Size G/6 (4 mm) crochet hook
or size needed to obtain gauge

ADDITIONAL
Stitch markers

LEARN BY VIDEO
www.go-crafty.com
- ch (chain)
- Changing colors
- Crocheting in the round
- dc
- hdc
- sc
- sc2tog
- sl st (slip stitch)

MEASUREMENTS
Approx 8¼" [21.5 cm] long.

GAUGE
15 sc and 16 rows = 4" [10 cm].
Take time to check gauge.

SPECIAL STITCH
Scbp Insert hook from back to front to back around post of sc. Yoh and draw through both loops on hook.

INSTRUCTIONS
Cocoa Section
With B, ch 15.

1st rnd: 1 sc in 2nd ch from hook. 1 sc in each of next 12 ch. 3 sc in last ch. Working into opposite side of ch, 1 sc in each of next 12 ch. 2 sc in last ch. Join with sl st to first sc. 30 sc.

2nd rnd: Ch 1. 1 sc in same sp as last sl st. 1 sc in each of next 13 sc. 3 sc in next sc. 1 sc in each of next 14 sc. 3 sc in last sc. Join with sl st to first sc. 34 sc.

3rd rnd: Ch 1. 1 sc in same sp as last sl st. 1 sc in each of next 14 sc. 3 sc in next sc. 1 sc in each of next 16 sc. 3 sc in next sc. 1 sc in last sc. Join with sl st to first sc. 38 sc.

4th rnd: Ch 1. 1 sc in same sp as last sl st. 1 sc in each of next 14 sc. 2 sc in next sc. 3 sc in next sc. 2 sc in next sc. 1 sc in each of next 16 sc. 2 sc in next sc. 3 sc in next sc. 2 sc in next sc. 1 sc in last sc. Join with sl st to first sc. 46 sc.

5th rnd: Ch 1. 1 sc in same sp as last sl st. 1 sc in each of next 16 sc. 2 sc in next sc. 3 sc in next sc. 2 sc in next sc. 1 sc in each of next 20 sc. 2 sc in next sc. 3 sc in next sc. 2 sc in next sc. 1 sc in each of last 3 sc. Join A with sl st to first sc. 54 sc. Break B.

6th rnd: With A, ch 1. 1 sc in same sp as last sl st. 1 sc in each of next 19 sc. 3 sc in next sc, placing marker on center sc. 1 sc in each of next 26 sc. 3 sc in next sc, placing marker on center sc. 1 sc in each of last 6 sc. Join with sl st to first sc. 58 sc.

7th rnd: Ch 1. 1 scbp around post of same sc as last sl st. 1 scbp around post of each sc around. Join with sl st to first st. Move markers from 6th rnd to corresponding sts on 7th rnd. Fasten off.

Mug Section

1st row: With RS of Cocoa Section facing, join A with sl st in either marked sc. Sl st in next sc. Ch 1. 1 sc in same sp as last sl st. 1 sc in each of next 27 sc. Turn. Leave rem sts unworked.

2nd row: Ch 2. 1 hdc in each of first 2 sc. 1 sc in each of next 24 sc. 1 hdc in each of last 2 sc. Turn.

3rd row: Ch 1. Sc2tog. 1 sc in each st to last 2 sts. Sc2tog. Turn 26 sts.

4th to 6th rows: Ch 1. 1 sc in each st to end of row. Turn.

7th row: Ch 1. Sc2tog. 1 sc in each st to last 2 sts. Sc2tog. Turn. 24 sts.

8th to 12th rows: Ch 1. 1 sc in each st to end of row. Turn.

13th row: Ch 1. Sc2tog. 1 sc in each st to last 2 sts. Sc2tog. Turn. 22 sts.

14th row: Ch1. 1 sc in each st to end of row. Turn.

15th row: Ch 1. 1 sc in each of first 3 sc. 1 hdc in each of next 16 sc. 1 sc in each of last 3 sc. Turn.

16th row: Ch 1. 1 sc in each of first 4 sts. 1 hdc in each of next 14 hdc. 1 sc in each of last 4 sts. Turn.

17th row: Ch 1.1 sc in each st to last sc. 3 sc in last sc, then work sc evenly up side of Mug Section ending with sl st in marked st of Cocoa Section. With RS facing, join A with sl st in marked st at opposite side of Cocoa Section and work sc evenly down side, ending with 2 sc in first sc (corner) of 15th row. Fasten off.

HANDLE

With A, ch 18.

1st row: 1 sc in 2nd ch from hook. 1 sc in each ch to end of chain. Turn. 17 sc.

2nd row: Ch 1. Working into back loops only, 1 sc in each sc to end of row.

Fold Handle in half. Ch 1. Join 2nd row to rem loops of foundation ch by working 1 row of sc through both thicknesses across. Fasten off.

MINI MARSHMALLOW (MAKE 10)

With C, ch 3.

1st row: (Yoh and draw up a loop) 3 times in 3rd ch from hook. Yoh and draw through 6 loops on hook. Yoh and draw through rem 2 loops on hook. Fasten off, leaving a 4" [10 cm] end.

FINISHING

Sew Mini Marshmallows and Handle in position as shown in picture.

peachy dishcloth

YARN
Lily® Sugar'n Cream® (Solids 2.5 oz/70.9 g; 120 yds/109 m)
- 1 ball each in #00042 Tea Rose (MC), #01699 Tangerine (A), and #00084 Sage Green (B)

HOOK
Size G/6 (4 mm) crochet hook
or size needed to obtain gauge

ADDITIONAL
Stitch markers

LEARN BY VIDEO
www.go-crafty.com
- ch (chain)
- Crocheting in the round
- dc
- hdc
- sc
- sl st (slip stitch)
- tr

MEASUREMENTS
Approx 7½" [19 cm] long.

GAUGE
15 sc and 16 rows = 4" [10 cm].
Take time to check gauge.

NOTE
Ch 3 at beg of rnd or row counts as dc.

INSTRUCTIONS
Peach
With MC, ch 4. Join with sl st to form ring.

1st rnd: Ch 3. 11 dc in ring. Join with sl st to top of ch 3. 12 dc.

2nd rnd: Ch 3. 1 dc in same sp as last sl st. 2 dc in each dc around. Join with sl st to top of ch 3. 24 dc.

3rd rnd: Ch 3. 1 dc in same sp as last sl st. 1 dc in next dc. *2 dc in next dc. 1 dc in next dc. Rep from * around. Join with sl st to top of ch 3. 36 dc.

4th rnd: Ch 3. 1 dc in same sp as last sl st. 1 dc in each of next 2 dc. *2 dc in next dc. 1 dc in each of next 2 dc. Rep from * around. Join with sl st to top of ch-3. 48 dc.

5th rnd: Ch 3. 1 dc in same sp as last sl st. 1 dc in each of next 3 dc. *2 dc in next dc. 1 dc in each of next 3 dc. Rep from * around. Join A with sl st to top of ch-3. Break MC. 60 dc.

6th rnd: With A, ch 1. *2 sc in next dc. 1 sc in each of next 4 dc. Rep from * around. Join with sl st to first sc. Break A. 72 sc.

Side of Peach
Join MC with sl st to 8th sc of previous rnd. Ch 1. 1 sc in same sp as sl st. 1 hdc in next sc. 1 dc in each of next 2 sc. 1 tr in next sc. (2 tr in next sc. 1 tr in each of next 5 sc) twice. 2 tr in next sc. 1 tr in next sc. 1 dc in each of next 2 sc. 1 hdc in next sc. 1 sc in next sc. Break MC. Do not turn. 26 sts.

Edging
Join A with sl st to 7th sc of 6th rnd. Ch 1. 1 sc in same sp as sl st. Working across side of Peach: (1 sc in each of next 6 sts. 2 sc in next

st) 3 times. 1 sc in each of last 5 sts. 1 sc in next sc of 6th rnd. Sl st in next sc. Fasten off.

FINISHING
Hanging Loop
With 2 strands of B held tog, join with sl st to top of Peach. Ch 12. Join with sl st in same sp as first sl st. Fasten off.

Leaf
With B, ch 12.
1st row: 1 sc in 2nd ch from hook. 1 hdc in next ch. 1 dc in next ch. 1 tr in each of next 5 ch. 1 dc in next ch. 1 hdc in next ch. 3 sc in last ch. Working across opposite side of ch, 1 hdc in next ch. 1 dc in next ch. 1 tr in each of next 5 ch. 1 dc in next ch. 1 hdc in next ch. 2 sc in last ch. Join with sl st to first sc. Fasten off.
Sew Leaf to Peach near Hanging Loop.

flower dishcloth

YARN
Lily® Sugar'n Cream® (Solids 2.5 oz/70.9 g; 120 yds; Ombres 2 oz/56.7 g; 95 yds/86 m)
- 1 ball each in #01740 Hot Pink or #01742 Hot Blue or #02739 Over the Raibow (MC); and #00010 Yellow (A)

Note: 1 ball each of MC and A will make 2 dishcloths.

HOOK
Size H/8 (5 mm) crochet hook
or size needed to obtain gauge

▶ LEARN BY VIDEO
www.go-crafty.com
- ch (chain)
- Crocheting in the round
- dc
- FPdc
- sc (single crochet)
- sl st (slip stitch)

MEASUREMENTS
Approx 9" [23 cm] in diameter.

GAUGE
13 sc and 14 rows = 4" [10 cm].
Take time to check gauge.

SPECIAL STITCHES
FPdc Yoh and draw up a loop around post of next st at front of work inserting hook from right to left. (Yoh and draw through 2 loops on hook).

NOTE
Dishcloth may be worked following text or chart.

INSTRUCTIONS
With A, ch 4. Join with sl st in first ch to form a ring.

1st rnd: Ch 1. 8 sc in ring. Join with sl st to first sc.

2nd rnd: Ch 1. Working in back loops only, 2 sc in each sc around. Join with sl st to first sc. 16 sc.

3rd rnd: Ch 1. Working in back loops only, 1 sc in first sc. Ch 1. (1 sc in next sc. Ch 1) 15 times. Join with sl st to first sc. Fasten off.

4th rnd: Join MC with sl st to any sc. Ch 3 (counts as dc). Working in both loops, (1 dc. Ch 2. 2 dc) in same sc as last sl st. Skip next ch-1 sp. 1 dc in next sc. Skip next ch-1 sp. *(2 dc. Ch 2. 2 dc) in next sc. Skip next ch-1 sp. 1 dc in next sc. Skip next ch-1 sp. Rep from * 6 times more. Join with sl st to top of ch 3.

5th rnd: Sl st in next dc and ch-2 sp. Ch 3 (counts as dc). (2 dc. Ch 2. 3 dc) in same sp as last sl st. Ch1. Skip next 2 dc. FPdc in next dc. Ch 1. Skip next 2 dc. *(3 dc. Ch 2. 3 dc) in next ch-2 sp. Ch 1. Skip next 2 dc. FPdc in next dc. Ch 1. Skip next 2 dc. Rep from* 6 times more. Join with sl st to top of ch 3.

6th rnd: Sl st in next dc. Ch 3 (counts as dc). 1 dc in next dc. (2 dc. Ch 2. 2 dc) in next ch-2 sp.

1 dc in each of next 2 dc. Ch 1. Skip next dc and ch-1 sp. FPdc in next dc. Ch 1. Skip next ch-1 sp and dc. *1 dc in each of next 2 dc. (2 dc. Ch 2. 2 dc) in next ch-2 sp. 1 dc in each of next 2 dc. Ch 1. Skip next dc and ch-1 sp. FPdc in next dc. Ch 1. Skip next ch-1 sp and dc. Rep from * 6 times more. Join with sl st to top of ch 3.

7th rnd: Sl st in next dc. Ch 3 (counts as dc). 1 dc in each of next 2 dc. 5 dc in next ch-2 sp. 1 dc in each of next 3 dc. Ch 1. Skip next dc and ch-1 sp. FPdc in next dc. Ch 1. Skip next ch-1 sp and dc. *1 dc in each of next 3 dc. 5 dc in next ch-2 sp. 1 dc in each of next 3 dc. Ch 1. Skip next dc and ch-1 sp. FPdc in next dc. Ch 1. Skip next ch-1 sp and dc. Rep from * 6 times more. Join with sl st to top of ch 3. Fasten off. ■

STITCH KEY
◯ = chain (ch)
• = slip st (sl st)
+ = single crochet (sc)
† = double crochet (dc)
= front post double crochet (FPdc)
⌒ = work in back loop only

pineapple dishcloth

YARN
Lily® Sugar'n Cream® (Solids 2.5 oz/70.9 g; 120 yds/109 m)
- 1 ball each in #01628 Hot Orange (MC) and #101222 Country Green (A)

Note: 1 ball of MC will make 2 dishcloths.

HOOK
Size H/8 (5 mm) crochet hook
or size needed to obtain gauge

LEARN BY VIDEO
www.go-crafty.com
- ch (chain)
- Changing colors
- dc
- dc2tog
- hdc
- sc
- sc2tog
- sl st (slip stitch)
- tr

MEASUREMENTS
Approx 7" x 12" [18 x 30.5 cm].

GAUGE
13 sc and 14 rows = 4" [10 cm].
Take time to check gauge.

NOTES
1 To join new color, work to last 2 loops on hook. Draw new color through last 2 loops then proceed in new color.
2 Pineapple may be worked from text or chart.

INSTRUCTIONS
With MC, ch 17.

1st row: (RS). 1 dc in 4th ch from hook (counts as 2 dc). *4 dc in next ch. Re-insert hook into first dc of 4-dc group and pull loop through. Ch 1 to close st— popcorn made. 1 dc in each of next 2 ch. Rep from * 3 times more. 14 sts. Turn.

2nd row: Ch 1. 1 sc in first dc. *2 sc in next dc. 1 sc in each of next 2 sts. Rep from * 3 times more. 2 sc in last dc. Turn. 19 sts.

3rd row: Ch 3 (counts as dc). *Popcorn in next sc. 1 dc in each of next 3 sc. Rep from * 3 times more. Popcorn in next sc. 1 dc in last sc. Turn.

4th row: Ch 1. 1 sc in each sc to end of row. Turn.

5th row: Ch 3. 1 dc in each of next 2 sc. *Popcorn in next sc. 1 dc in each of next 3 sc. Rep from * 3 times more. Turn.

6th row: As 4th row.

7th to 17th rows: Rep 3rd to 6th rows twice more, then rep 3rd to 5th rows once.

18th row: (WS). Ch 1. 1 sc in first dc. *Draw up a loop in each of next 2 sts. Yoh and draw through all loops on hook— sc2tog made. 1 sc in each of next 2 sts. Rep from * 3 times more. Sc2tog. Turn. 14 sts.

19th row: Ch 3. * Yoh and draw up a loop in next st. Yoh and draw through 2 loops on hook) twice—dc2tog made. Popcorn in next sc. Rep from * 3 times more. 1 dc in last sc. Turn. 10 sts.

20th row: Ch 1. 1 sc in each st to end of row. Join B. Break MC. Turn.

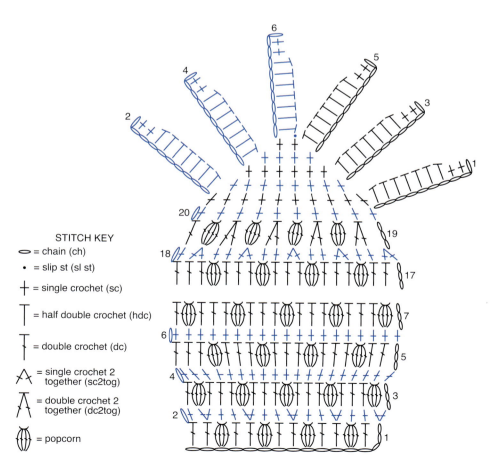

STITCH KEY
- ⌒ = chain (ch)
- • = slip st (sl st)
- + = single crochet (sc)
- T = half double crochet (hdc)
- ┬ = double crochet (dc)
- ⋀ = single crochet 2 together (sc2tog)
- ⋀ = double crochet 2 together (dc2tog)
- ⬭ = popcorn

Leaves

1st row: (RS). With B, ch 10. 1 sc in 2nd ch from hook. 1 sc in next ch. 1 hdc in each of next 7 ch. 1 sc in each of next 10 sc. Turn.

2nd row: Ch 10. 1 sc in 2nd ch from hook. 1 sc in next ch. 1 hdc in each of next 7 ch. Skip next sc. 1 sc in each of next 8 sc. Turn. Leave rem sc unworked.

3rd row: Ch 10. 1 sc in 2nd ch from hook. 1 sc in next ch. 1 hdc in each of next 7 ch. Skip next sc. 1 sc in each of next 6 sc. Turn. Leave rem sc unworked.

4th row: Ch 10. 1 sc in 2nd ch from hook. 1 sc in next ch. 1 hdc in each of next 7 ch. Skip next sc. 1 sc in each of next 4 sc. Turn. Leave rem sc unworked.

5th row: Ch 10. 1 sc in 2nd ch from hook. 1 sc in next ch. 1 hdc in each of next 7 ch. Skip next sc. 1 sc in each of next 2 sc. Turn. Leave rem sc unworked.

6th row: Ch 10. 1 sc in 2nd ch from hook. 1 sc in next ch. 1 hdc in each of next 7 ch. Skip next sc. Sl st in next sc. Fasten off.

primrose **dishcloth**

YARN
Lily® Sugar'n Cream® (Solids 2.5 oz/70.9 g; 120 yds/109 m)
- 1 ball or 33 yds/30 m in #01628 Hot Orange (A)
- 1 ball or 66 yds/ 60 m in #01111 Mod Blue (B)

HOOK
Size H/8 (5 mm) crochet hook
or size needed to obtain gauge

LEARN BY VIDEO
www.go-crafty.com
- ch (chain)
- Crocheting in the round
- dc
- sc
- sl st (slip stitch)

MEASUREMENTS
Approx 8½" [21.5 cm] in diameter.

GAUGE
13 dc and 7 rows = 4" [10 cm].
Take time to check gauge.

NOTE
Ch 2 at beg of each rnd does not count as stitch.

INSTRUCTIONS
With A, ch 2.

1st rnd: 10 dc into 2nd ch from hook. Join with sl st to first dc.

2nd rnd: Ch 2. 2 dc in each of next 10 dc. Join B with sl st to first dc. 20 dc.

3rd rnd: With B, ch 2. *1 dc in next dc. 2 dc in next dc. Rep from * around. Join with sl st to first dc. 30 dc.

4th rnd: Ch 2. *1 dc in next dc. 2 dc in each of next 2 dc. 1 dc in next dc. 1 sc in next dc. Rep from * around. Join with sl st to first dc. 42 sts.

5th rnd: Ch 2. *1 dc in each of next 2 dc. 2 dc in each of next 2 dc. 1 dc in each of next 2 dc. 1 sc in next sc. Rep from * around. Join with sl st to first dc. 54 sts.

6th rnd: Ch 2. *1 dc in each of next 3 dc. 2 dc in each of next 2 dc. 1 dc in each of next 3 dc. 1 sc in next sc. Rep from * around. Join with A with sl st to first dc. 66 sts.

7th rnd: With A, ch 2. 1 dc in each of next 3 dc. 2 dc in each of next 4 dc. 1 dc in each of next 3 dc. 1 sc in next sc. Join with sl st to first dc. 78 sts.

Hanging loop
Sl st in each of next 6 dc. Ch 8 for loop. Join with sl st in same sp as last sl st. Fasten off.

stripey star **dishcloth**

YARN
Lily® Sugar'n Cream® (Solids 2.5 oz/70.9 g; 120 yds/109 m)
- 1 ball each in #00095 Red (A), #00001 White (B), and #00009 Bright Navy (C)

HOOK
Size H/8 (5 mm) crochet hook
or size needed to obtain gauge

LEARN BY VIDEO
www.go-crafty.com
- ch (chain)
- Crocheting in the round
- dc
- hdc
- sl st (slip stitch)

MEASUREMENTS
Approx 11" [28 cm] from point to point.

GAUGE
13 sc and 14 rows = 4" [10 cm].
Take time to check gauge.

INSTRUCTIONS
With A ch 4. Join with sl st to form ring.

1st rnd: Ch 3 (counts as dc). 9 dc in ring. Join with sl st to top of ch 3. 10 dc.

2nd rnd: Ch 2 (counts as hdc). (1 hdc. Ch 2. 2 hdc) in same sp as last sl st. Skip next dc. *(2 hdc. Ch 2. 2 hdc) in next dc. Skip next dc. Rep from * around. Join B with sl st to top of ch 2.

3rd rnd: With B, sl st in next hdc. Ch 2 (counts as hdc). *(2 hdc. Ch 2. 2 hdc) in next ch-2 sp. 1 hdc in next hdc. Skip next 2 hdc. 1 hdc in next hdc. Rep from * 3 times more. (2 hdc. Ch 2. 2 hdc) in next ch-2 sp. 1 hdc in next hdc. Skip next 2 hdc. Join C with sl st to top of ch 2.

4th rnd: With C, sl st in next hdc. Ch 2 (counts as hdc). 1 hdc in next hdc. *(2 hdc. Ch 2. 2 hdc) in next ch-2 sp. 1 hdc in each of next 2 hdc. Skip next 2 hdc. 1 hdc in each of next 2 hdc. Rep from * 3 times more. (2 hdc. Ch 2. 2 hdc) in next ch-2 sp. 1 hdc in each of next 2 hdc. Skip next 2 hdc. Join B with sl st to top of ch 2.

5th rnd: With B, sl st in next hdc. Ch 2 (counts as hdc). 1 hdc in each of next 2 hdc. *(2 hdc. Ch 2. 2 hdc) in next ch-2 sp. 1 hdc in each of next 3 hdc. Skip next 2 hdc. 1 hdc in each of next 3 hdc. Rep from * 3 times more. (2 hdc. Ch 2. 2 hdc) in next ch-2 sp. 1 hdc in each of next 3 hdc. Skip next 2 hdc. Join A with sl st to top of ch 2.

6th rnd: With A, sl st in next hdc. Ch 2 (counts as hdc). 1 hdc in each of next 3 hdc. *(2 hdc. Ch 2. 2 hdc) in next ch-2 sp. 1 hdc in each of next 4 hdc. Skip next 2 hdc. 1 hdc in each of next 4 hdc. Rep from * 3 times more. (2 hdc. Ch 2. 2 hdc) in next ch-2 sp. 1 hdc in each of next 4 hdc. Skip next 2 hdc. Join B with sl st to top of ch 2. Cont as established, working 1 more hdc before each (2 hdc. Ch 2. 2 hdc) group and working 1 rnd each of B, C, B and A. Fasten off. ■

ribbon flower **dishcloth**

YARN
Lily® Sugar'n Cream® (Solids 2.5 oz/70.9 g; 120 yds/109 m)
- 1 ball or 44 yds/40 m in #00010 Yellow or #01628 Hot Orange or #01215 Robin's Egg (MC
- 1 ball or 9 yds/ 8 m in #00001 White (A)

Note: 1 ball each of MC and A will make 2 dishcloths.

HOOK
Size H/8 (5 mm) crochet hook
or size needed to obtain gauge

ADDITIONAL
- 6 stitch markers
- Length of satin ribbon ⅛" [3 mm] wide

LEARN BY VIDEO
www.go-crafty.com
- ch (chain)
- Crocheting in the round
- dc
- sc
- sl st (slip stitch)

MEASUREMENTS
Approx 8" [20.5 cm] in diameter.

GAUGE
13 sc and 14 rows = 4" [10 cm].
Take time to check gauge.

NOTE
1 Ch 2 at beg of each rnd does not count as dc.
2 Dishcloth may be worked from text or chart.

INSTRUCTIONS
With MC, ch 4. Join with sl st to first ch to form a ring.

1st rnd: Ch 2. 10 dc in ring. Join with sl st to first dc.

2nd rnd: Ch 2. 2 dc in each of next 10 dc. Join with sl st to first dc. 20 dc.

3rd rnd: Ch 2. *2 dc in next dc. 1 dc in next dc. Rep from * around. Join with sl st to first dc. 30 dc.

4th rnd: Ch 2. *1 dc in next dc. 2 dc in each of next 2 dc. 1 dc in next dc. 1 sc in next dc. Rep from * around. Join with sl st to first dc. 42 sts.

5th rnd: Ch 2. *1 dc in next dc. 2 dc in each of next 2 dc. 1 dc in each of next 3 dc. 1 sc in next sc. Rep from * around. Join with sl st to first dc. 54 sts.

6th rnd: Ch 2. *1 dc in each of next 3 dc. 2 dc in each of next 2 dc. 1 dc in each of next 3 dc. 1 sc in next sc. Rep from * around. Join A with sl st to first dc. 66 sts.

7th rnd: With A, ch 1. 1 sc in same sp as last sl st. *2 sc in each of next 8 dc. 1 sc in next dc. 1 sc in next dc 4 rows below. Place marker on last sc. 1 sc in next dc. Rep from * around, omitting sc at end of last rep. Join with sl st to first sc. Fasten off.

Thread satin ribbon through all marked sc. Pull tightly and tie in a bow. ■

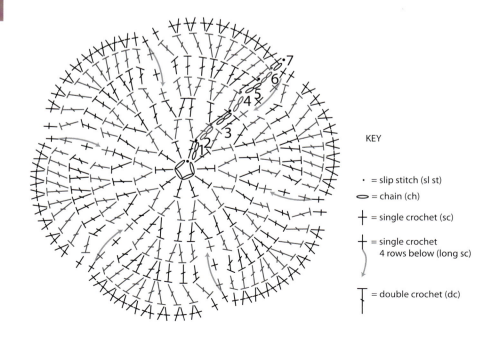

KEY

· = slip stitch (sl st)
◯ = chain (ch)
+ = single crochet (sc)
+ = single crochet 4 rows below (long sc)
T = double crochet (dc)

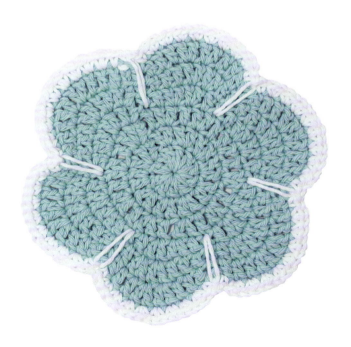

basic striped dishcloth

YARN
Lily® Sugar'n Cream® (Solids 2.5 oz/70.9 g; 120 yds/109 m)
- 1 ball each in #01223 Mod Green or #02744 Swimming Pool (A)
- 1 ball each in #01215 Robin's Egg or #00001 White (B)

HOOK
Size H/8 (5 mm) crochet hook
or size needed to obtain gauge

ADDITIONAL
Tapestry needle

LEARN BY VIDEO
www.go-crafty.com
- Basic stripes
- ch (chain)
- Changing colors
- sc (single crochet)
- sl st (slip stitch)

MEASUREMENTS
Approx 8" x 8" [20.5 cm x 20.5 cm].

GAUGE
13 sc and 14 rows = 4" [10 cm]. *Take time to check gauge.*

NOTE
1 When joining colors, work to last 2 loops on hook of first color. Draw new color through last 2 loops and proceed.
2 When joining a new color, leave a tail approximately 4 inches [10 centimeters] long to ensure you are left with enough yarn to weave in your end.

INSTRUCTIONS
With A, chain 30.

1st row: 1 single crochet (sc) in 2nd chain from hook. *Chain (ch) 1. Skip next ch. 1 sc in next ch. Repeat from * to end of ch. Turn. (You should have 15 sc and 14 chain-1 spaces (ch-1 sps) at end of row).

2nd row: Ch 1. 1 sc in first sc. *1 sc in next ch-1 space. Ch 1. Skip next ch. Repeat from * 10 times more. 1 sc in next ch-1 sp. 1 sc in last sc. Join B (see note). Turn. (You should have 16 single crochet and 13 ch-1 sps at end of row).

3rd row: With B, ch 1. 1 sc in first sc. *Ch 1. Skip next sc. 1 sc in next ch-1 sp. Repeat from * to last 2 sts. Ch 1. Skip next sc. 1 sc in last sc. Turn. (You should have 15 sc and 14 ch-1 sps at end of row.)

4th row: As 2nd row. Join A (see note). Turn.

5th row: With A, as 3rd row.

Repeat 2nd to 5th rows for pattern until work from beginning measures 8" [20.5 cm], ending with 2 rows of either color.

Fasten off. ■